THE BEST WEIRD WORLD RECORDS

meadowside CHILDREN'S BOOKS

MOST FINGERS AND TOES

At an inquest held on a baby boy at Shoreditch in the East End of London, UK, on 16 September 1921 it was reported that he had 14 fingers and 15 toes.

FASTEST WIFE CARRIER

The fastest time to complete the 235-m (771-ft) obstacle course of the World Wife-Carrying Championships, held annually in Sonkajärvi, Finland, is 55.5 sec by Margo Uusorg and Birgit Ulricht of Läänernaa, Estonia, on 1 July 2000.

FASTEST FURNITURE

The 'Casual Lofa', a motorized sofa built by Edd China and David Davenport, has a top speed of 140 km/h (87 mph). Powered by a Mini 1300-cc engine, it is licensed for use on UK roads and is steered by turning a medium-sized pizza pan.

MOST UNDERWATER ROPE JUMPS IN ONE HOUR

The record for the most underwater rope jumps in one hour is 900 and was set by Ashrita Furman (USA) at the Gurney's Inn pool in Montauk, New York, USA, on 23 August 2001.

HEAVIEST WEIGHT LIFTED BY EAR

The heaviest weight lifted using only the ear is 50 kg (110.1 lb) by Li Jian Hua of Jiangshan, China. He lifted a column of bricks hanging from a clamp attached to one of his ears and held the weight for 9.3 sec on 17 December 1998 at the studios of *Guinness World Records: Primetime* in Los Angeles, California, USA.

MOST VALUABLE HAIR

The most valuable hair clippings sold at auction are a mass of dark black cuttings from the head of Elvis Presley. They were sold by his personal barber, Homer 'Gill' Gilleland, for $115,120 (£72,791) to an anonymous buyer during an online auction held by MastroNet Inc, Oak Brook, Illinois, USA, on 15 November 2002.

38

HEAVIEST VEHICLE PULLED BY HAIR

The heaviest vehicle to have been pulled by the hair alone over a distance of 32.85 m (107 ft 9.5 in) is a double-decker bus weighing 7,874 kg (17,359 lb). It was pulled by Letchemanah Ramasamy of Selangor, Malaysia, at Bruntingthorpe Proving Ground, Leicestershire, UK, on 1 May 1999.

BATH SITTING WITH THE MOST SNAKES

Jackie Bibby of Fort Worth, Texas, USA, and Rosie Reynolds-McCasland of Granbury, Texas, USA, jointly hold the record for sitting in a bathtub with the most live rattlesnakes. Bibby and Reynolds-McCasland sat in two separate tubs, each with 75 Western Diamondback rattlesnakes, on the set of *Guinness World Records: Primetime* on 24 September 1999 in Los Angeles, California, USA.

752KG

HEAVIEST BED OF NAILS SANDWICH

Lee Graber of Tallmadge, Ohio, USA, was sandwiched between two beds of nails, with a weight of 752.5 kg (118 st 7 lb) placed on top, for a total of 10 sec on 24 June 2000. This is considered the heaviest weight possible, and Guinness World Records will no longer accept claims for this record!

LONGEST TIME SPENT ON A BED OF NAILS

The duration record for non-stop lying on a bed of nails is 274 hr 2 min by Inge Wilda Svingen, ending on the *Good Morning Norway* programme on 3 November 1984.

LARGEST BANANA COLLECTION

The International Banana Club Museum in Altadena, 32 km (20 miles) north of Los Angeles, California, USA, has 17,000 banana-related articles on display. The museum was opened in 1972 and has 9,000 members in 27 countries.

LARGEST BARBIE DOLL COLLECTION

Tony Mattia of Brighton, East Sussex, UK, has collected 1,125 Barbie dolls – about one half of the range of Barbie models ever produced since 1959, including many versions of her boyfriend Ken.

ATTCHOOO!
ELVIS
CHARLES
DICKENS
MONROE
LINCOLN
EINSTEIN

LARGEST COLLECTION OF HAIR FROM HISTORICAL FIGURES

John Rezinkoff of Connecticut, USA, has accumulated a collection of hair from 115 different historical figures. This collection of famous locks is insured for $1 million and includes genuine tresses from the heads of Abraham Lincoln, John F. Kennedy, Marilyn Monroe, Albert Einstein, Napoleon, Elvis Presley, King Charles I and Charles Dickens.

LARGEST GNOME AND PIXIE COLLECTION

Since 1978, Ann Atkin, of West Putford, North Devon, UK, has collected a total of 2,010 gnomes and pixies, all of which 'live' in her four-acre Gnome Reserve. The Reserve enjoys an average of 25,000 visitors per year who are encouraged to wear hats and temporarily become gnomes for their magical journey through the woodland.

LONGEST MOUSTACHE

The moustache of Kalyan Ramji Sain (India) has been growing since 1976, and by July 1993 had reached a span of 3.39 m (11.1 ft) – the right side 1.72 m (5.6 ft) and the left side 1.67 m (5.4 ft).

CIRCUS

LONGEST NOSE

There are historical accounts stating that Thomas Wedders, who lived in England during the 1770s and was a member of a travelling circus, had a nose measuring 19 cm (7.5 in) long.

TALLEST TRUE GIANT

The world's tallest recorded true (non-pathological) giant was Angus MacAskill, UK, born on the island of Berneray in the Sound of Harris, Western Isles. He stood 2.36 m (7 ft 9 in) tall and died in St Anne's, Cape Breton Island, Nova Scotia, Canada. His record was officially recognized by Queen Victoria, who awarded him two gold rings for being the strongest and tallest man to visit Windsor Castle.

MOST EXTREME CASE OF MUNCHAUSEN'S SYNDROME

The most extreme recorded case of the rare and incurable condition known as 'Munchausen's syndrome' (a continual desire to have medical treatment) was Irish-born Stewart McIlroy, who cost the National Health Service an estimated £2.5 million during his 50-year career as a hospital patient. During that time, he had 400 major and minor operations, and stayed at 100 different hospitals using 22 aliases.

MOST VARIABLE STATURE

The only person in medical history to have been both a dwarf and a giant is Adam Rainer of Graz, Austria, who holds the record for the most variable stature. Rainer measured a petite 1.18 m (3 ft 10.5 in) at the age of 21 but suddenly started growing rapidly. Within 10 years, he had stretched to 2.18 m (7 ft 2 in) but became so weak that he was bedridden for the rest of his life. When he died in 1950, aged 51, he measured a lofty 2.34 m (7 ft 8 in) tall.

NAO PERTURBE
DO NOT DISTURB
FORSTYRR IKKE
NE PAS DÉRANGER
PLEASE DO NOT DISTURB
NO PERTURBE
STÖREN SIE NICHT
DO NOT DISTURB
QUIET PLEASE
NE PAS DÉRANGER
STOOR NIET
NO MOLESTAR
DISTURB NOT

LARGEST COLLECTION OF 'DO NOT DISTURB' SIGNS

Swiss accountant Jean Francois Vernetti holds the record for the largest collection of 'Do Not Disturb' signs, having amassed 2,195 notices from 131 different countries.

LARGEST COLLECTION OF AIRSICKNESS BAGS

Niek Vermeulen of The Netherlands holds the record for the largest collection of airplane sick bags – a stomach-churning 3,307. It is believed that the airsickness bag was invented sometime in the 1920s on a particularly turbulent flight from Moscow to Berlin.

LONGEST BANZAI SKYDIVE

Banzai skydiving involves throwing a parachute out of an aeroplane and then jumping after it. The aim is obvious: to grab the parachute, strap it on and open it. The record for the longest Banzai skydive is held by Japan's Yasuhiro Kubo, who flung his parachute out of plane flying at 3,000 m (9,842.5 ft) and caught up with it 50 sec later on 2 September 2000 at Davis, California, USA.

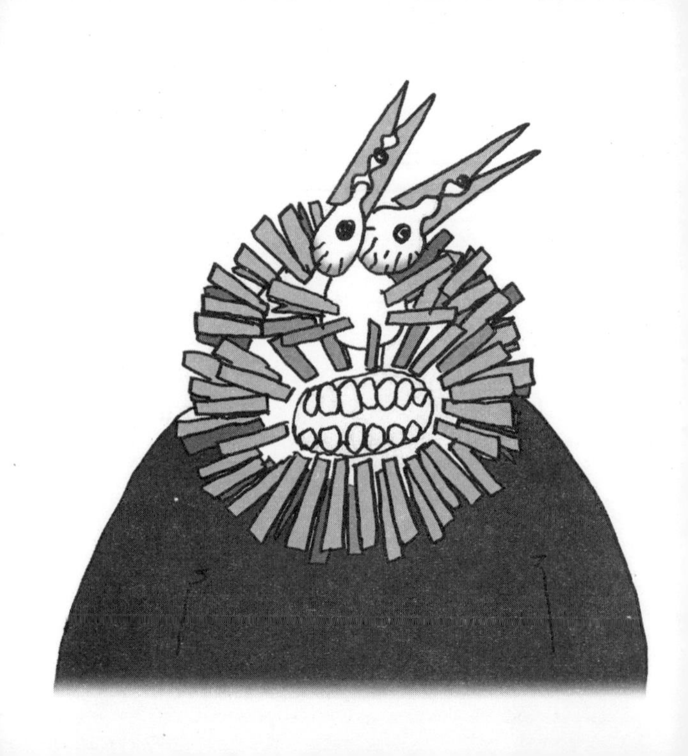

MOST CLOTHES PEGS CLIPPED TO FACE

Garry Turner, UK, clipped 133 ordinary wooden clothes pegs on his face at the offices of *Guinness World Records*, London, on 3 August 2001.

HEAVIEST CONCRETE BLOCK-BREAK ON A BED OF NAILS

Ciro Gallo (UK) had 37 concrete blocks weighing a total of 235.8 kg (519.8 lb) placed on his chest and then broken with a 6.35 kg (14 lb) sledgehammer while he lay on a bed of nails at Marlowes, Hemel Hempstead, Hertfordshire, UK, on 24 August 2002.

LARGEST FEET

If cases of elephantiasis are excluded, then the biggest feet currently known are those of Matthew McGrory of Pennsylvania, USA, who wears size 28½ US shoes (UK size 28).

MOST TATTOOED MAN

Tom Leppard and Lucky Rich, who both live in the UK, share the record for having the most tattoos. The area of their bodies covered is approximately 99.9 per cent. Tom, who resides on the Isle of Skye in Scotland, has opted for a leopard skin design, with all the skin between the dark spots tattooed saffron yellow. Lucky Rich has had his existing tattoos blacked over, with a white design tattooed on top.

LARGEST UNDERWATER PRESS CONFERENCE

On 20 June 1997, a group of 12 journalists representing Spanish newspapers and TV dived to a depth of 16 m (52 ft 5 in), off El Hierro, Canary Islands, to be present at the 20 min book launch of *Champion's Secrets* – an underwater photo manual written by Carlos Virgili Ribé.

LONGEST LIVED TWO-HEADED COW

The longest time a two-headed cow has lived is 17 months 15 days. Gemini, a heifer Holstein calf, was born on 4 August 1991 on Russell and Perry Stowells' Farm in Woodland, Michigan, USA, weighing 340 kg (749 lb) and died on 19 January 1993.

MOST WEIGHT LIFTED WITH EARS, NIPPLES AND TONGUE

The most weight simultaneously lifted using the ears, tongue and nipples is 13.19 kg (29.1 lb) held by Joe Hermann, USA, a member of the Jim Rose Circus. On 25 September 1998, he successfully lifted two standard 1.04 kg (2.3 lb) steam irons with his earlobes, picked up a 2.26 kg (5 lb) car battery with his tongue and supported the weight of a 7.12 kg (15.7 lb) cinderblock from his nipples.

LONGEST BEARD ON A WOMAN

Vivian Wheeler of Wood River, Illinois, USA, grew a full beard after the death of her mother in 1990. The longest strand from the follicle to the tip of hair was measured at 27.9 cm (11 in) in 2000. The longest female beard ever belonged to 'bearded lady' Janice Deveree of Kentucky, USA, and grew an incredible 36 cm (14 in).

LARGEST COLLECTION OF SQUATTING FIGURINES

As of March 2000, Spain's Guillem Duran I Suner had handmade 2,000 individually unique Catalan figures known as Caganers. A Caganer is a small hand-painted terracotta or ceramic figure in an obvious defecating posture. These figurines are a traditional part of the Catalan Christmas nativity scene.

FASTEST TIME TO SMASH A PIANO

The record time for demolishing an upright piano with sledge hammers and passing the entire wreckage through a circle 22.8 cm (9 in) in diameter is 1 min 37 sec by six members of the Tinwald Rugby Football Club, Ashburton, New Zealand, led by David Young on 6 November 1977.

KG

LARGEST RUBE GOLDBERG

Twelve students at the Monache High School, Porterville, California, USA, constructed a machine built to give you change in 50 pennies from two quarters using a total of 113 different steps. The entire process included using a flushing toilet, the head of a doll, an empty bottle of stout and a rubber chicken. A Rube Goldberg machine is one that will accomplish a simple everyday task in the most complicated manner possible.

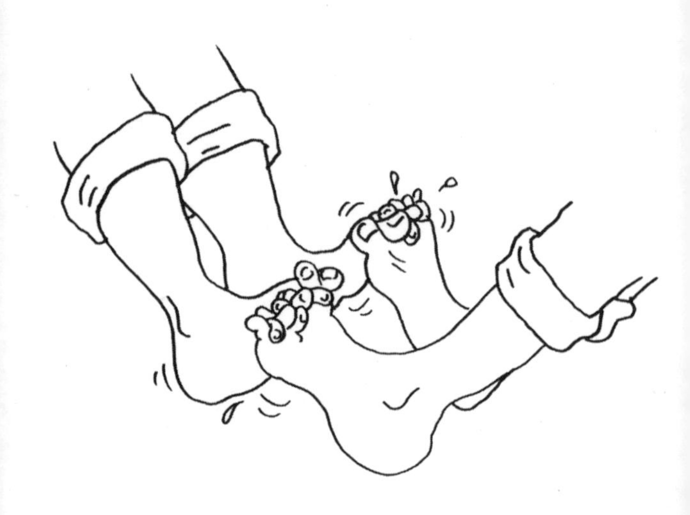

MOST MEN'S TOE WRESTLING WORLD CHAMPIONSHIPS

The most Toe Wrestling World Championships won in the Men's category is five by Alan Nash, UK. Nash, nicknamed 'Nasty', also has the honour of being knighted by His Majesty King Leo I of Redonda in the West Indies.

MOST CARS WRECKED

Over a period of more than 40 years up until his retirement in 1993, Dick Sheppard of Gloucester, UK, wrecked a total of 2,003 cars – not because he was a bad driver but because it was his profession and hobby as a stuntman.

HOTTEST METAL IN THE MOUTH

Yim Byung Nam held in his mouth for 14 sec a piece of metal that had been heated to a temperature of 487.7°C (910°F) on the set of *Guinness World Records: Primetime* in Los Angeles, California, USA, on 18 December 1998.

DEEPEST SCUBA DIVE BY A DOG

Dwane Folsom (USA) regularly takes his dog, Shadow, scuba diving off the coast of Grand Cayman Island. The deepest the pair usually go is approximately 4 m (13 ft). When diving, Shadow wears a specially adapted diving suit made up of a helmet, weighted dog jacket and breathing tube connected to his owner's air tank.

MOST STRAWS STUFFED IN THE MOUTH

Marco Hort of Switzerland stuffed 222 drinking straws in his mouth, holding them there for 10 sec on the *Barbara Karlich Show* (ORF 2, Vienna, Austria) on 11 March 2003.

OLDEST BRIDESMAID

Flossie Bennett, at the age of 97 years 181 days, was Matron of Honour at the wedding of Leonard and Edna Petchey on 6 February 1999 at St Peter's Church, Holton, East Anglia, UK. The only other woman asked to take part in the marriage ceremony was Leonard's 12-year-old granddaughter – an 85 year age gap between the two bridesmaids!

MOST PROLIFIC CRYING STATUE

A 40-cm (15.75-in) plaster statue of the Virgin Mary, bought from the Marian shrine at Medjugorje, Bosnia and Herzegovina, by an Italian curate in 1994 was given to the Grigori family in Civitavecchia, Italy. Between 2 February and 17 March 1995, the statue appeared to cry tears of blood on 14 occasions, including one manifestation witnessed by the diocesan bishop.

MOST THREATENED RELIGION

As of May 2003, only six members of the United Society of Believers in Christ's Second Appearance (Shakers) remain. They live in a small community near New Gloucester, Maine, USA.

LONGEST PERIOD OF STIGMATISM

Padre Pio (Francesco Forgione), a devout Italian Capuchin friar, bore the stigmata (the wounds received by Christ on the Cross) from 1918 until his death in 1968. The wounds were seen by thousands of pilgrims. Padre Pio was beatified on 2 May 1999 and canonized on 16 June 2002 by Pope John Paul II.

STRANGEST DIET

Michel Lotito of Grenoble, France, known as Monsieur Henri Mangetout, has been eating metal and glass since 1959. Gastroenterologists have X-rayed his stomach and have described his ability to consume 0.9 kg (2 lb) of metal per day as unique.

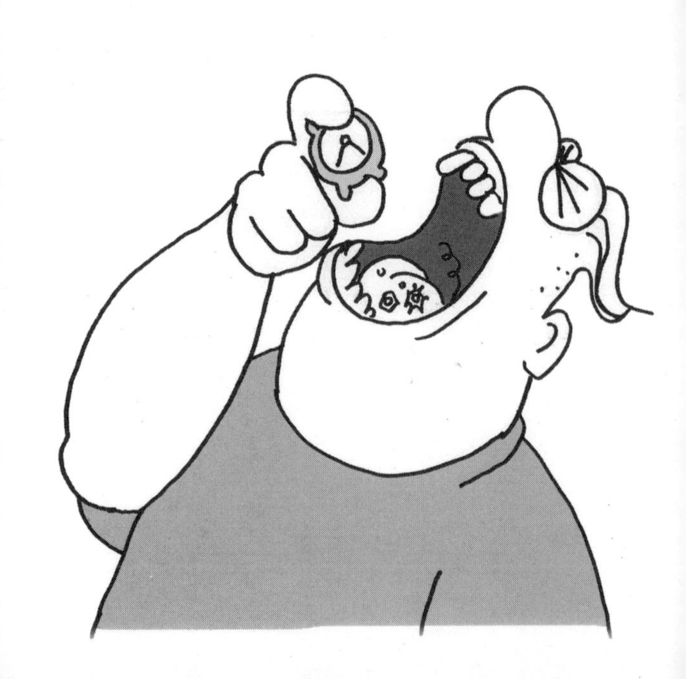

MOST WATCHES EATEN

Kim Seung Do from Seoul, South Korea, ate five watches (the entire watch with the exception of the wristband) in 1 min 34.07 sec on 18 December 1998 on the set of *Guinness World Records: Primetime* in Los Angeles, California, USA.

31

FARTHEST NIRA (JAPANESE CHIVE) THROWING

The distance record for nira (Japanese chive) throwing, as per the rules of 'nira-tobashi' competitions held at the Sako Festival in Kochi-ken, Japan, is 11.11 m (36 ft 5 in) by Junsuke Miyamoto of Kochi-ken on 20 June 1997.

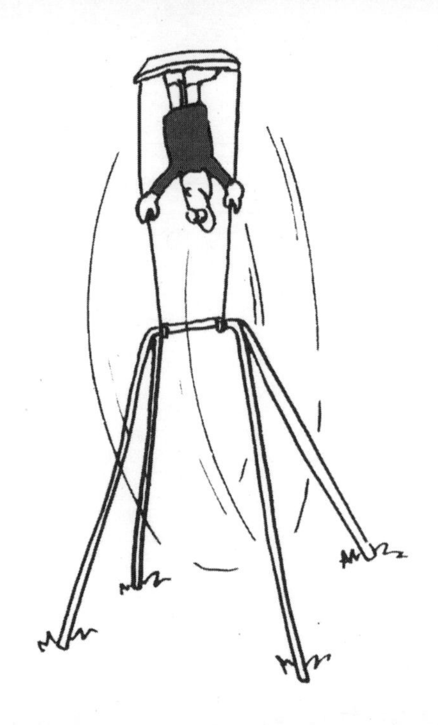

LONGEST KIIKING SHAFT SUCCESSFULLY ACHIEVED

Kiiking is a sport in Baltic and Scandinavian countries where the aim is to complete a 360-degree revolution on a swing. The record is based on the length of the shafts for the swing, so the longer the better. The longest shaft used to successfully complete a rotation in kiiking is 7.01 m (23 ft) by Andrus Aasamäe from Estonia at Rakveres, Estonia, on 16 July 2000.

PUBLICATION CONTAINING THE MOST USELESS INVENTIONS

Chindogu comes from the Japanese for 'weird tool' and has been popularized by designer and anarchist Kenji Kawakami. It is the art of inventions which, at first sight, appear to be useful but, upon closer inspection, reveal their utter uselessness. Kawakami has published two books containing *Chindogu* inventions. Examples include tiny dusters that slip onto a cat's paws, enabling it to clean dusty surfaces as it walks around!

Cartoons by:
Guy Harvey

Designed and edited by:
Jon Richards, Ed Simkins

For Guinness World Records:
Claire Folkard, Craig Glenday, Kim Lacey, Christian Marais

Printed in India